To witness that, to be present,
as this unbelievable story took place,
to be allowed to accompany these musicians from oblivion, literally,
to a standing ovation on the stage of Carnegie Hall,
that was a gift and a privilege without equal,
and at the same time a unique lesson in dignity and humility,
for us and for future generations.

Wim Wenders

Wim and Donata Wenders

BUENA VISTA SOCIAL CLUB

THE BOOK OF THE FILM

The best of the film stills and
many additional photographs by Wim and Donata Wenders

Autobiographical statements by
Compay Segundo, Ibrahim Ferrer, Rubén González
and the others

The well-known songs in the Spanish original
and in English translation

With a Foreword by Wim Wenders
and an Interview with Ry Cooder

Thames & Hudson

All the black-and-white photographs in the book were taken by Donata Wenders
and the panoramic colour photographs by Wim Wenders.
All the other reproductions are stills from the film.

The publishers are grateful to Wendy Burton for her crucial encouragement
and inspiration, and to Denise Booth, Marc Hertling and Marc Klocker
for their generous help and support during the preparation of this book.

The song lyrics are reproduced with kind permission of the following publishers:
Candela by Faustino Oramas (Termidor Musikverlag GmbH & Co. KG)
Chan Chan by Francisco Repilado (Termidor Musikverlag GmbH & Co. KG)
Cienfuegos by Victor Lay (Termidor Musikverlag GmbH & Co. KG)
Dos Gardenias by Isolina Carillo (Peer Musikverlag GmbH)
El Carretero by Guillermo Portabales (Peer Musikverlag GmbH)
Silencio by Rafael Hernandez (Peer Musikverlag GmbH)
Veinte Años by María Teresa Vera (carimusic corporation with kind permission of Wintrup Musik)
¿Y Tú Qué Has Hecho? by Eusebio Delfín (Termidor Musikverlag GmbH & Co. KG)

The film subtitles used in the book were translated from the Spanish by Michael Donnelly.
The Foreword was translated from the German by Philip Watson and revised by Wim Wenders.
Translations of the song lyrics and biographies from the Spanish and German
were provided by Michelle Beaver, Francisca Garvie and Philip Watson.
Peter Kemper's interview with Ry Cooder is reproduced with kind permission
of the *Frankfurter Allgemeine Zeitung*.

This edition first published in the United Kingdom in 2000 by
Thames & Hudson Ltd, 181A High Holborn, London WC1V 7QX

www.thamesandhudson.com

British Library Cataloguing-in-Publication Data
A catalogue record for this book is available from the British Library

ISBN 0-500-28220-X

Printed and bound in Italy

Contents

Foreword

Wim Wenders

I had never been to Havana before,
never shot a documentary film,
not even a concert,
and certainly never fully digital …
I wasn't really prepared for what we were up to.
And that was a good thing.

But one thing was for sure: I liked this music,
ever since I first heard it,
unmixed, unfinished, on a demo tape,
long before it came out on CD.
When I think about it,
this film had already begun then,
two years before we started shooting,
driving through Los Angeles at night.
Ry had given me this tape without saying much,
as is his way, and without a big introduction.
'Check this out', he said, 'This is what I recorded in Cuba.'
Totally unprepared, I listened for the first time, in my car,
to *Chan Chan* and *Dos Gardenias* and all the others songs …

This music was like nothing I ever heard before.
It was comforting like a hot bath
and refreshing like a cold shower.
It was as infectious and lively as it was wise and soothing.
Listening to it for the first time,
I couldn't possibly know,

what sort of contagious effect this music would have on my life.
But it dawned on me, that I was going to be addicted.
In fact years later I still listen to it almost every day.

So here was the main reason for making this film:
To find out what sort of people could make that kind of music.
I asked Ry, of course, the next day,
but the more I learned from him
about Compay, Ibrahim, Omara or Rubén,
the more my curiosity would grow.
I couldn't stop thinking about what he told me
about Havana as well,
or rather, *how* he told me about Havana.
The enthusiasm in his voice,
That gleam in his eyes
whenever he went back there in his mind …

To discover this city,
with it its music,
and those who sang and played it ...
For two years that remained a secret dream.

I didn't have much more than this dream in mind
when we actually flew to Havana in February 1998.
Ry hadn't given me much more than a week's notice
to prepare myself for the journey.
'Remember? You said you wanted to come with me
the next time I went to Cuba.
Well, we're flying over next week.
We want to make a second album,
with Ibrahim as lead singer.'

That challenge – 'Are you coming or not?' –
was exactly the right approach
to make sure I wasn't going to backtrack.
So I had just one week to assemble a crew,
and to scrape together some money.
As for giving any thought to *what* I wanted to film in Havana,
there simply wasn't time.
'Concepts are for sissies.'

On the plane to Mexico I was scared stiff.
My little crew was due to arrive a day later from Germany.
We would have to start filming first thing the following morning.
Ry didn't have much more than two weeks to produce the album.
And that would be all the time we had for the filming.
(Little did I know that I would still be shooting
two months later, in Amsterdam,
and another two months later in New York ...)

My German crew was made up of just two members:
Martin Müller as sound engineer, always ready for any adventure,
(we had worked together numerous times ever since
Alice in the Cities) and Jörg Widmer as cameraman.
Jörg had worked as Steadicam operator on *Faraway, So Close!*
and had left a great impression on me.
His instrument, the Steadicam,
is one heck of a heavy and bulky piece of equipment,
but Jörg was actually able to dance with it, to swirl around
and tango with a fifty-kilo load strapped around him,
and to make it look easy.

Basically these were the only decisions that I had taken for the film:
not to shoot on film, but to use a digital camera instead,
and not to put the camera on a tripod,
but to have it move around constantly, fluidly.
Right or wrong, there was no going back on those decisions.
We were about to start.
In addition to the Digi-Beta that Jörg was going to bring
   from Germany,
I had brought along my two little Sony Mini-DVs.
If this 'consumer technology'
could somehow be combined with the professional camera,
and cut together, in the end, I didn't know.
And nobody could tell us.

I didn't know much anyway.
That became painfully clear to me on the flight to Mérida.
I only knew one thing, my mantra, as it were:
The music should speak for itself.
Not what *I* thought about it should be of any importance,
or how *I* felt about these people I was going to meet.
No, they should be heard themselves,
together with their extraordinary music.

The smaller my crew, the better our chance of becoming invisible.
Along with camera operator and sound man
Donata came along as photographer,
Rosa Bosch would join us as production manager,
and the ICAIC would help us with a Cuban location manager,
plus perhaps, if necessary, a translator.
My Spanish was rusty.

In a booth at Mérida airport, Donata and I
had to sort out our Cuban visas and tickets for the onward flight.
In the United States
we had only been able to buy plane tickets for Mexico.
For the USA, Cuba was still non-existent.
Struck off the map.
The Buena Vista Social Club's Grammy award several weeks
    earlier
for 'Best Latin American Recording'
had been quite a sensation.
The first sign of a new awareness?

We arrived in Havana that evening.
Even on the road from the airport into town
it dawned on us 'newcomers' that things were going to be
different here.

Everything was dark, to begin with.
Streets and houses shrouded in the deep darkness of the night.
In the meagre light of the few cars
shadows flurried across the footpaths,
and some tired dogs crossed the streets.
Coming from Los Angeles, where the night is mostly lit up as
    bright as day,
it was striking to realize that neon lights and electricity
had suddenly turned into luxury items.
One thing was obvious right away,
You could feel it physically:
A different timescale prevailed here.
We got to know the Cuban Time better over the next few weeks.
It was like no other time I knew.
Or was it? Like a time I had known in my childhood perhaps?

The American cars from the fifties
rattled around everywhere like mythological motor-driven beings
straight out of my childhood dream of 'America'.
And weren't we in the middle of America, after all?

In an old movie palace called 'America' in old Havana
there was a giant mosaic on the floor of the foyer,

hidden under a layer of dust, like everything here.
It showed a large-scale map of North and South America.
In the middle, nestling in the big bay between the two
  half-continents,
like a baby between its parents, or like a seed in the ground,
lay Cuba.
Havana was the centre of gravitation in this map.

The city of Havana was one vast hand-coloured picture postcard.
I've never seen colours like this anywhere else.
As a child I collected postcards,
from foreign countries, with foreign stamps.
Most weren't colour photos,
but black-and-white ones with the colour added afterwards.
That hand-coloured surface of Havana,
All those layers of paint peeling off,
made the city appear as if under a spell, caught and frozen in time.

Everything lay there as 'in perfect tranquillity',
and at the same time one had the feeling that some war had just
  ended.
Whole streets were broken up and destroyed as if by bombing
  raids.

But it wasn't just cars and houses in ruins
That reminded me of childhood, of forgotten times.
Those were just the surface, the foreground.
But from within the city, from its very heart,
something revealed itself more and more, the longer we stayed.
It was in the eyes.
Everyone you met looked you openly in the face.
Hardly ever a dark look,
never once a jealous or resentful one.
Instead, cheerful eyes from morning till evening:

every smile was met with a smile in reply.
The language here, the language of eyes, was sheer friendliness,
honesty and directness were the rules of the game.

The little eight-year-old ballerina who came running after us
to give us back the twenty-dollar bill
that must have fallen from Donata's bag ...
she knew just how many hours her father had to work for that
  money.
But my wife never even had time to say thank you,
as the girl was off again, with a satisfied smile.
And we both stood there, with tears in our eyes.
That little event summed up so many of our feelings
about this city and its people.

Sometimes, especially during the long editing process,
it seemed to me as if I had only been hazily aware of it all,
of Havana and Cuba,
as if my crew and I had not been able to see as clearly
as we would have wanted to.
As if somehow we didn't quite have the right
to see everything as it was,
we people from the future, from 1998,
from the age of over-information,
used to consuming anything and everything, our eyes and
  stomachs full ...
We saw everything from the point of view of our own timescale,
certainly through our digital cameras.
(With her black-and-white photos and her old Leica
Donata was in closer touch with Cuban time.)

Looking back, it seems that the only thing I saw and perceived
  clearly
– after all, what I had *wanted* to see in the first place

and what we had come here to discover –
were the people who made this music.

In the end, each of them had grown in my view, in our hearts,
to proportions 'larger than life'.
Already during the filming it dawned on me
that we weren't so much making a documentary,
as a character piece.
We had discovered a story and we were following it.
Compay, Ibrahim, Rubén, Omara, Eliades, Pío and the others
were the leading actors in this story,
more the 'principal characters', if I may put it like that,
than 'just themselves'.

Only this story was true.
(And so, of course, it wasn't really a story at all.)

It told of the unbroken spirit of these people,
who despite all the disappointments and the knocks they had
   survived
had never given up,
and who also weren't going to let the success and world fame
which had caught some of them at a biblical age
(Compay was over ninety when we made the film)
throw them off track.

The musicians of the Buena Vista Social Club
owe their rediscovery
to Juan de Marcos, Nick Gold and above all to Ry Cooder.
I owe it to him
for taking me on this journey.

Thanks, Ry.

Compay Segundo

Vocal, Guitar

'Ah, the Buena Vista Social Club!
We need to ask the older folks
in the neighbourhood:
"Hey, where was the
Buena Vista Social Club?"'
Compay looks around searchingly.
'Where are the old folks?
We're looking for the Social Club.'

PASSER-BY   'The Buena Vista Social Club?
Oh, that. That's long gone.'

ANOTHER   'The Buena Vista was, let's see ...'

ANOTHER   'We've lived here since 1944.
I remember the guy who used to
throw the parties at the Social Club.
In its day, the best bands
in Cuba played there.'

COMPAY   'When I drink too much,
you know what I eat?
Black *cocoquetta* soup.
Consommé, chicken consommé.
You take a piece of chicken neck,
then you fry it up.
Just when it's no longer bloody,
you toss in chopped garlic.
Anyone who eats that will have
no aches or pains.
I hate hangovers.
That's how I stay fit.'

Chan Chan

De Alto Cedro voy para Marcané
Luego a Cueto voy para Mayarí.

El cariño que te tengo
Yo no lo puedo negar
Se me sale la babita
Yo no lo puedo evitar.

Cuando Juanica y Chan Chan
En el mar cernían arena
Como sacudía el ›jibe‹
A Chan Chan le daba pena.

Limpia el camino de paja
Que yo me quiero sentar
En aquel tronco que veo
Y así no puedo llegar.

De Alto Cedro voy para Marcané
Luego a Cueto voy para Mayarí.

Chan Chan

From Alto Cedro I'm going to Marcané
And then from Cueto I'm going to Mayarí.

The love I have for you
I cannot deny;
My mouth is watering
I just can't help it.

When Juanica and Chan Chan
Sifted sand together on the beach,
How her bottom shook!
How Chan Chan was aroused!

Clear the path of dry cane leaves;
I want to sit down
On that tree trunk over there,
Otherwise I won't make it.

From Alto Cedro I'm going to Marcané
And then from Cueto I'm going to Mayarí.

Ry Cooder

Guitar

'My son Joachim and I came back down here to Havana
in March 1998. We'd been here before, two years ago,
recording the *Buena Vista Social Club*.

'I've been making records about thirty-five years,
and I can tell you,
you never know what the public is going to go for.
This turned out to be the one they liked the best.
I like it the best.

'One of the great things about that record
turned out to be Ibrahim Ferrer.
He'd come in off the street like a Cuban Nat King Cole.
You stumble on somebody like this maybe once in your life.
We wanted to try recording with him.
A solo record.
Let him be heard.'

Silencio

Duermen en mi jardín
Las blancas azucenas,
Los nardos y las rosas.
Mi alma muy triste y pesarosa
A las flores quiere ocultar su amargo dolor.

Yo no quiero que las flores sepan
Los tormentos que me da la vida.
Si supieran lo que estoy sufriendo
Por mis penas llorarían también.

Silencio, que están durmiendo
Los nardos y las azucenas.
No quiero que sepan mis penas
Porque si me ven llorando
Morirán.

Hush!

Sleeping in my garden
Are the white lilies,
Spikenards and roses.
My soul so sad and sorrowful
Wants to hide its bitter pain in the flowers.

I don't want the flowers to know about
The torments that life throws at me.
If they knew what I am suffering
They too would weep for my sorrows.

Hush! For they are sleeping,
The spikenards and lilies.
I don't want them to know about my sorrows
Because if they see me weeping
They will die.

Ibrahim Ferrer

Vocal

'I, Ibrahim Ferrer Planas
was born in a small town
near Santiago de Cuba, in San Luis.
I am the son of Aurelia Ferrer.
Registered as her natural son.
I say this because
I'd like you all to know
from me what I am and how I am.

'At age twelve I lost my mother.
I had already lost my father.
I was orphaned
as the only child she had.
So, I had to plunge into life.
Just like my friends, I was in school
but I had to abandon
my studies at that time.
Because life,
naturally, wasn't as it is now.
It was harder.
One had to go out and find it.'

Dos Gardenias

Dos gardenias para tí
Con ellas quiero decir:
Te quiero, te adoro, mi vida
Ponle toda tu atención
Porque son tu corazón y el mío.

Dos gardenias para tí
Que tendrán todo el calor de un beso
De esos besos que te dí
Y que jamás encontrarás
En el calor de otro querer.

A tu lado vivirán y se hablarán
Como cuando estás conmigo
Y hasta creerás que te dirán:
Te quiero.
Pero si un atardecer
Las gardenias de mi amor se mueren
Es porque han adivinado
Que tu amor me ha traicionado
Porque existe otro querer.

Two Gardenias

Two gardenias for you
With which I want to say:
I love you, adore you, my life.
Give them your whole attention,
For they are your heart and mine.

Two gardenias for you
With all the warmth of a kiss,
Like those kisses I gave you
And which you will never know
In the hot embrace of another.

They will live beside you
And talk to you as I do.
You'll even believe they're telling you:
'I love you.'
But if late one evening
My love's gardenias should die,
It's because they have discovered
That you have betrayed me
Because you love another.

Omara Portuondo

Vocal

'My name is Omara Portuondo.
I was born here, in a section of Havana.
In the neighbourhood called Cayo Hueso.

'My mother and father
used to relax just after lunch.
Then they would sing songs. Duets.
That's when I began to love
our Cuban music.
For example, *La Bayamesa*.
I began singing that one
when I was just a young girl,
with my father singing the lead voice,
and me the back-up.
And this same song, *Veinte Años*,
which I recorded here
on the Grammy-winning album,
I've also known since I was a child.'

Veinte Años

¿Qué te importe que te amé
Si tú no me quieres ya?
El amor que ya ha pasado
No se debe recordar.

Fuí la ilusión de tu vida
Un día lejano ya
Hoy represento al pasado
No me puedo conformar
Hoy represento al pasado
No me puedo conformar.

Si las cosas que uno quiere
Se pudieran alcanzar
Tu me quisieras lo mismo
Que veinte años atrás.

Con qué tristeza miramos
Un amor que se nos va.
Es un pedazo del alma
Que se arranca sin piedad.

Twenty Years

What does it matter that I love you
If you no longer love me?
The love that is past
Must not be reawakened.

I was your life's desire
Once so long ago.
Now I represent the past
And I can't face up to that.
Now I represent the past
And I can't face up to that.

If all the things we wanted
Were to come within our grasp,
You would love me just the same
As twenty years ago.

We watch with so much sadness
A love that fades away.
It is a part of our souls
That is heartlessly torn out.

Compay Segundo

'I was born in 1907.
At the ocean's edge.
In Siboney.
I lived there with my father.
He was a machinist
on the mining trains.
The magnesium mines.
So, I was in Siboney until
I was about nine years old.
That's when my grandmother died.
Later, I would move to Santiago
with my brothers.
But I couldn't leave Siboney
until my grandmother died.
She put it this way:
"Until I die, my grandson ..."
(that's me)
"... cannot leave my side."
So, I'd light her cigars.
I was five years old.
She'd say,
"Here, light me a cigar."
I'd light it like this,
then hand it to Grandma, and she'd smoke it.
So, I guess you could say
that I've been smoking for eighty-five years ...

'As long as blood
runs in my body,
I'm going to love women.
Because in life, women, flowers
and romance are all so lovely.

'One night of romance ...
Oh, that has no price.
No price at all.
And I haven't yet forgotten how.
At my ninety years,
I have five children.
You met Salvador
and Basilio.
Salvador is the youngest.
I have five.
But right now,
I'm working on the sixth.
Now I want six.
One more.'

¿Y Tú Qué Has Hecho?

En el tronco de un árbol una niña
Grabó su nombre henchida de placer
Y el árbol conmovido allá en su seno
A la niña una flor dejó caer.

Yo soy el árbol conmovido y triste
Tu eres la niña que mi tronco hirió
Yo guardo siempre tu querido nombre
¿y tú, qué has hecho de mi pobre flor?

What Have You Done?

On the trunk of a tree a young girl
Joyfully carved out her name.
The tree, touched to the core,
Let fall a flower to the girl.

I am the tree, so sad and moved.
You are the girl who gashed my trunk.
I shall always treasure your dear name.
And you, what have you done with my poor flower?

Rubén González

Piano

'My name is Rubén González y Fontantillis.
I was born in the city of Santa Clara, in Las Villas,
in the year 1919.
At age seven, I began to study piano,
a piano that the family had purchased.
A very fine piano, a John Stowers piano.
It was also a player piano.
It sounded very lovely.
So when I saw that instrument,
I went crazy.
I really liked it.
I used to play a lot on it.
So, I began to study and study.
When it seemed I had the potential
to become a great piano player,
Mom had me take lessons with a private teacher
from Cienfuegos.

'So, I started with her
in the first grade.
Then the second, the third, the fourth, the fifth …
until the eighth grade.
That's when she told me:
"Rubén, you're going to be a good pianist.
You have great skill with your hands."

'So, we moved from Santa Clara to Havana.
There, in Havana … I felt somewhat dubious.
"There are a lot of piano players in Havana",
I thought to myself.
So, I began to study other things
as much as I could.

'As it turned out,
in the house next to mine there lived a person
whom I later came to know as Arsenio.
He had formed a great band.
And he heard me play.
But he was blind.
He wasn't born that way,
but he'd had an accident
and lost his sight.
Anyway, one day Arsenio says to me:
"Rubén, would you like to play with my group?"
And I said, "Yes, of course."
The pianist who was with him
had gone somewhere else.
To Europe.
So he left me his gig.
I played with Arsenio some four years.
I had a lot of hits.'

Eliades Ochoa

Guitar

'I am Eliades Ochoa Bustamante.
I was born in Santiago de Cuba
on 22 June 1946.
My mother, Jacoba Bustamante,
played the *tres*
and my father played the *tres*.
A musical family.
I was born a country boy, of course.
From the time I awoke in the morning,
I began listening to music.
Besides having music in my blood,
I heard music night and day.

'In 1958, I was the same size as a guitar.
I started playing as a kid
all around Santiago.
In the red light district,
I played and passed the hat:
"Pitch in with Cuban musicians!"
That's how I made my money,
which I took home
to help out my parents.'

El Carretero

Por el camino del sitio mío
Un carretero alegre pasó
Con sus canciones que es muy sentida
Y muy guajira alegre cantó:

Me voy al transbordador
A descargar la carreta
Me voy al transbordador
A descargar la carreta
Para cumplir con la meta
De mi penosa labor.

A caballo vamo' pa'l monte.

Yo trabajo sin reposo
Para poderme casar
Yo trabajo sin reposo
Para poderme casar
Y si lo llego a lograr
Seré un guajiro dichoso.

A caballo vamo' pa'l monte.

Yo soy guajiro y carretero
Y en el campo vivo bien
Porque el campo es el edén
Más lindo del mundo entero
Chapea el monte, cultiva el llano
Recoge el fruto de tu sudor.

The Cart Driver

Along the track by my house
A merry cart driver passed.
With his deeply sentimental songs
In his jolly, rustic way he sang:

I'm going to the crossing
To unload my cart,
I'm going to the crossing
To unload my cart,
And so get to the end
Of my back-breaking work.

Let's ride our horses to the mountain.

I work without rest
So that I can get married.
I work without rest
So that I can get married.
And if I can manage that
I'll be a happy country fellow.

Let's ride our horses to the mountain.

I am a country lad and cart driver
And I live well on the land,
Because the countryside is Eden,
The most perfect place on earth.
Till the mountain, cultivate the plain,
Reap the fruits of your toil.

Ibrahim Ferrer

'My mother was a firm believer in this Lazarus,
which is the same one that I carry everywhere.
I believe strongly in my Lazarus.
They call him the Beggar.
He is a powerful figure.
He's the one who opens paths,
the one who helps the disempowered, you might say.
The other Lazarus, the Bishop, is an equal,
but this Lazarus is the one I have in me.
The one who asks for alms.
I place flowers for him.
Every so often, I light him a candle.
I give him honey.
Here, look! I give him bee honey. Here.
A lot of perfumes. That's for sure. A lot of perfume.
Every time I leave, I spray him,
and I spray myself, too.
His little shot of rum.
Naturally, because I like it,
I suppose he does, too.
So, he gets his little rum gifts.

'Sometimes my wife
makes him a meringue.
Do you know what that is?
She makes him one of those,
and we place it here for him.
We dedicate it to him.
And so that's how his things
come to him.

'We Cubans can be thankful,
rather, we can give thanks to
Who knows?
Maybe to that Man up there
that we are like this, because
if we'd followed the way of possessions
we would have disappeared long ago.
We Cubans are very fortunate.
In that regard we are very small,
but, well, we are strong.
We have learned to resist
both the good and the bad.'

IBRAHIM   'I was dumped.
I stayed home; I lost touch.
Am I going to starve to death?
No! I'll shine shoes.
I'll collect trash, or whatever.
I'll sell lottery tickets.
I mean, I have my children, a family to support.
I'm not ashamed to say that.

'I swear, I'm not going to smoke any more.
Honest. Well, only a little anyway.
Very little, you understand.
And drinking? No more of that either.'
Points to his wife.
'You see, I've got,
well, a bodyguard here
who, after all, just won't let me.'

RY COODER   'It's 1998,
we have to do the best we can.
So we have Ibrahim in 1998.
We're very lucky.'

IBRAHIM   'Thank you, thank you.'

RY COODER   'Very, very lucky!'

IBRAHIM   'The one thing I don't want is to die.
At least, not right now. Please!
That Man up there, and my wife
over there, ought to grant me ...
Points to his wife.
... at least a bit more time
to enjoy this some more.
Because, you know, sometimes they don't give you any.'

RY COODER   'You always have to ask, who wrote it,
and are they still living.
In case they may be here or they come down,
get them to come down.
More people, you know, have died,
but so many are left,
so we always want to try to find those people.
You know, they might be down the street,
they might be here, who knows,
they might be around the corner. You never know.'

Ibrahim Ferrer

'One afternoon they knocked on my door.
They had come looking for me at home.
It was Juan de Marcos.
I was shining some shoes at the time.
He says, "What are you doing, now?"
"Me?" I say. "Well, I'm just here,
shining some shoes and all."
Then he says, "No, no, I'm looking for you."
"Why? To do what there?"
"Come with me."
"No, I don't want to sing any more", I told him.
"No, man, I need your voice. No one else can do it."
So I ask him,
"When will this be? Tomorrow?"
"No, right now", he says.
"Well, at least let me shower ..."
"No, no, right now", he said.
He pressured me so hard, I was only able to wash my face
and wipe off a little shoe polish.
So we came here, to the Egrem.
Here, in the Egrem studios, I found Eliades de Ochoa.
When he saw me, he was with Compay Segundo and others.

Rubén was there, on piano. When he saw me,
he began playing a number
which I had made very popular here in Cuba.
It's called *Candela*,
a composition by Faustino Oramas, "El Guayabero".
So, I start in:

A rat put on a dance
to make great merriment.
A mouse played the kettle-drum,
enlivening the fields for a day.
A cat also came along,
all elegant and affable.
"Good evening, my friend", he said ...

'"It goes like that", I tell him.
So I started to sing the number.
And Ry was in the booth;
it seems he had his eye on me.
He heard me
and decided to record the song.
I figured, "Alright, no problem."
So we recorded it.'

Cienfuegos

CORO: Cienfuegos tiene ya su guaguancó.

Hoy siento gran emoción.
Voy a cantarle a mi tierra:
A esa famosa región
llamada »perla sureña«.

Su mujer es un primor
radiante como una estrella
y por su elegante andar
la admiran en Cuba entera.

Cienfuegos, yo a tí te llevo
metido en mi corazón
por eso con orgullo
te doy esta inspiración.

CORO: Ya tú lo ves, mi hermano,
Cienfuegos tiene su guaguancó ...

Cienfuegos

CHORUS: Cienfuegos has got its own guaguancó sound.

Today I'm feeling deep emotion,
Wanting to sing the praises of my homeland:
That famous region
Known as the 'Pearl of the South'.

Woman there is exquisite,
Radiant as a star,
And for the elegant way she walks,
All Cuba admires her.

Cienfuegos, I carry you
Deep within my heart,
And that is why with pride
I offer you this inspiration.

CHORUS: Now you will see, my brother,
Cienfuegos has its own guaguancó sound ...

Pío Leyva and
Manuel Licea, 'Puntillita'

Vocals

PÍO   'I am Pío Leyva,
the Cuban Highlander.'

PUNTILLITA   'I am Manuel Licea, "Puntillita".
Here's the cure for you.'

PÍO   'A blank one ...
and, Domino!'
Can't you see, I'm a phenomenon?
I'm telling you, you can't beat me, Puntillita,
because, at dominoes, I'm number one.
Singing, you may be the best,
but at dominoes I'm the ultimate!'

Candela

Ay candela, candela, candela me quemo aé.
Puso un baile un jutía, para una gran diversión.
De timbalero un ratón, que alegraba el campo un día.
Un gato también venía, elegante y placentero ...
Ay candela, candela, candela me quemo aé.
Oye, Faustino Orama' y sus compañeros,
   necesito que me apaguen el fuego.
Margarita llama pronto a los bomberos
   para que vengan a apagar el fuego.
Tilán tilán
Didilán didilán
Margarita que me quemo
Yo quiero seguir gozando
La candela me está llevando
Me gusta seguir guarachando
Esta tarde venimo' acabando
Como quiera venimo' tocando
La mujer cuando se agacha
Se le abre el entendimiento
Y el hombre cuando lo mira
Se le para el pensamiento

Fire

Oh, fire, fire, fire, I'm burning!
A rat put on a dance to make great merriment.
A mouse played the kettle-drum, enlivening the fields for a day.
A cat also came along, all elegant and affable ...
Oh, fire, fire, fire, I'm burning!
Listen, Faustino Oramas and friends,
   I need someone to put out the flames.
Margarita, call the firemen quickly,
   to come and put out the flames.
Tilán, tilán,
Didilán, didilán,
Margarita, I'm on fire:
I want it to go on.
The fire is carrying me off:
I want it to continue.
This afternoon will be time to end.
We'll go on acting as we like.
When a woman bends over
She opens up her mind,
And when a man looks at her
His brain shuts down.

De tí me gusta una cosa
Sin que me cueste trabajo
De la barriga pa'rriba, de la cintura pa'bajo
Mira se quema, se quema, mama
Mira mama que me quemo
Mira se quema Báyamo, mira que Songo está que arde
Mira se quema La Maya, mira ese pito que suena.
Malaguën está que corta mama
Santiago de Cuba está que te mete en llamas
Se quema, se quema, se quema, oye, mira me quemo,
  me quemo.
Mira que me quemo, oye, yo quiero seguir guarachando.
Mira mama que yo vengo quemando.
Faustino Orama' tú está acabando
Mira se quema, se quema
Pero mira mi mami se quema
Oye se quema, se quema.

There's one thing I like about you
Which isn't hard to see:
It's from the belly up and from the waist down.
Look, it's burning, burning, Mama;
Look, Mama, I'm burning.
Look, Báyamo's burning; look, Songo is in flames.
Look, La Maya is burning; hear the whistle blowing.
Malaguën is in trouble, Mama;
Santiago de Cuba can set you on fire.
It's burning, burning, burning; listen, look, I'm burning,
  burning.
Look, I'm burning; listen, I want it to continue.
Look, Mama, I'm catching fire.
Faustino Oramas, you're getting near the end.
Look, it's burning, burning,
But look, Mama, it's burning.
Listen, it's burning, burning.

Barbarito Torres

Laúd

'I am Bárbaro Alberto Torres Delgado.
In musical jargon, I'm known as "Barbarito". Barbarito Torres.
Since I was a child, from age ten,
I've played Cuban provincial music.

'I play an instrument called the *laúd*,
which originates from Arabia.
The Moors took it to Spain,
where it underwent its first metamorphosis.
There, they made the *laúd* with a longer neck,
a little larger than the one used here.
Troubadours brought the instrument here to Cuba,
where it underwent its second metamorphosis.
That resulted in the Cuban *laúd*.
Which is the one that I play.'

Manuel Mirabel Vázquez

Trumpet

'My name is Manuel Mirabal Vázquez,
better know in the musical world
as "El Guajiro".
I started playing at age eighteen,
which means I've been playing trumpet for forty-seven years.
It was quite an experience
playing with all these *compañeros*.
All these folks were practically forgotten.
If Buena Vista hadn't emerged, nobody would remember
Ibrahim Ferrer, Rubén, Compay Segundo.
To see Compay at ninety, standing there, playing his *tres* so well,
and Rubén playing his piano so well,
I think they are great factors
in the success of this group.'

Amadito Valdés

Percussion

'I am Amadito Valdés,
percussionist.
I use my father's name
as he was my primary motivation
to follow this path.
In the field of percussion, the *timbale*
is a very limited instrument.
So, the person who plays it
must have a sense of how
to make the imagination dance,
using an instrument of such limitations
in its physical design.
It's a very docile instrument,
but one which undoubtedly lends a lovely colour
to popular dance music.'

Orlando López

Bass

'My name is Orlando López, "Cachaíto".
I'd like to tell you a bit about how
I began working in music.
I began when I was nine years old.
At eleven, I started playing with
an orchestra directed by my aunt,
Coralia López, another "Cachao".
Starting with my great-grandfather,
we were all bassists.
I was even going to study violin,
but my grandfather told me:
"No, it has to be bass."
It was, well, one of those things.

'I was a little afraid of the bass,
but it was a matter of adapting to it,
getting familiar with that instrument.
My style of playing is
to concentrate myself.
It's that, I like music so much.

'As I had worked in classical music,
and all other genres,
I feel, oh, I don't know ...
I guess playing music
is like a game.'

Joachim Cooder

Percussion

'For what I do, percussion, Cuba is the Mecca.
Viewed as nothing but pure musical energy.
The *uda* drum, which makes the dip,
the "goomp, goomp" sound,
they all got a big kick out of it last time,
so they would all laugh and say, "Ay, goomp, goomp."
So I became the guy with the funny sounds.
It's not anything obvious, because it fills a pocket,
that so much of the percussion
is going around the one of each bar
they usually leave out.
It adds up to I know what Ry kind of has in mind,
a strange departure
in a bizarre band that never existed
back in the sixties or something.
Puntillita took sort of an interest in teaching me stuff.
Like everyone is a percussionist,
and it's almost like those that aren't
are the best percussionists.
The ones who have that light touch
that's so hard to find.
There's no kind of learning like the kind of learning
that you get from the guys here.
It's so subtle and quiet,
and so powerful at the same time.'

Ry Cooder

Guitar

'My friend Nick Gold
of World Circuit Records in London
called me up, asked if I'd join him in Cuba.
Make a record of Cuban music
with some *campesino* musicians
and some West African players.
It sounded like a great idea
that had never been tried. Sure.
My wife and I had been in Havana in the seventies,
kind of poking around and
searching around for this soul music
from a tape a friend had given us.
It had some incredible playing
and some of the most beautiful songs on it.
I'd never heard anything like it,
so we'd got on a boat and went down there
and kind of snuck around and searched around,
and actually heard some good old-timers,
but I didn't know what to do about it in those days.
I didn't know how to proceed or pursue anything,
so we came back home,

and I've been thinking about it ever since.
When we got down this time,
Nick picked us up at the airport and said,
"You know the Africans couldn't make it.
They got hung up in Paris. What are we going to do here?"
So we figured we'd just go ahead
with whoever we could find.
So, we started asking around.
Juan de Marcos helped us out,
and pretty soon we had a room full of people,
including Compay Segundo,
Eliades Ochoa, Ibrahim Ferrer,
Amadito Valdés, Pío and Puntillita, Rubén,
Cachao and Barbarito Torres, who's the *laúd* player.
Turns out it was him on the tape
that I'd had all these years
that sort of lured me down there in the first place.
These were people that I'd heard on records for many years,
had no idea if they were living or dead.
Rubén Gonzales hadn't even had a piano in ten years.
He'd barely been playing.
They told us he had arthritis and couldn't play.
Of course that wasn't true.

'And this is an example of
the kind of luck and good fortune you have to have.
To find out that so many of these people
were still alive and well, although forgotten,
happy to play, very generous and open-hearted
with their talent and their knowledge.
It was a fantastic experience.
It was the kind of thing, it might be fair to say,
I trained for my whole life.

Something very rare.
I tell Joachim,
this might just happen to you once in your life.

'On the trip to LA, I started thinking
what a great thing it would be
to get everybody together and do a show someplace.
By that time the record had gotten so popular
that these guys were all really busy.
The only place we could get everybody together
was Amsterdam.

'Everybody knows Carnegie Hall is the place to go.
Cubans kept asking me:
"When we going to New York?"
I actually never thought it would happen,
but a lot of people worked hard, and tried really hard,
and on 1 July we were there.
That was a great night.
They loved it, I loved it, everybody just went crazy.
That would be the last show
for the Buena Vista Social Club.'

New York

Rubén and Eliades on the Empire State Building

RUBÉN 'The Statue of Liberty, where is it?'

ELIADES 'Over there.
With the big point on top.
Near those two towers there.
You saw it when we came in, yesterday.'

RUBÉN 'Near that tower over there?'

ELIADES 'No, this one over here.'

RUBÉN 'That can't be the Statue.
It's all by itself, on the point of an island.
Like that real tiny one down there,
only it's much bigger.
It seems to me that the Statue had a crown.'

ELIADES 'But you can't distinguish that from here.
You'd need to find a viewer,
or something to see it.'

RUBÉN 'Yeah, I guess that would be a problem.'

ELIADES 'From here, you can't see
if she's wearing a crown.'

RUBÉN 'No, I guess you'd have to get closer to see that.
But at least we know it's in that direction.'

ELIADES 'That, we do know.
Let's move into the sun.'

RUBÉN 'You want some sun? Let's go.'

ELIADES 'Rubén, have you ever been here before?'

RUBÉN 'Yes, many years ago.'

ELIADES 'Up here?'

RUBÉN 'Up here?
Oh, no, I went to the Statue.
From the Statue
we were looking down ...'

ELIADES 'How did you get there?'

RUBÉN 'With some people, some tourists.'

ELIADES 'That was in the 1920s, you said?'

RUBÉN 'The year?
I was about thirty; I'm eighty, now.'

Pío and Puntillita

PUNTILLITA 'Did you see what an amazingly beautiful
building that is? A marvel.'

PÍO 'What an enormous thing! An extraordinary thing.'

PUNTILLITA 'And the avenues are beautiful.'

PÍO 'Incredibly.'

PUNTILLITA 'This really is good. Very beautiful.'

PÍO 'Activity. Activity. Activity!
Look at the pistol that guy has.
Look, look over here!'
They stand in front of a window display.
'All the greats are there! You see? All the greats.'
Bet you don't know who ...'

PUNTILLITA 'There's Charlie Chaplin!'

PÍO 'Laurel and Hardy. Remember them?'

PUNTILLITA 'You're right! The Fat guy and the Skinny guy.'
Puntillita points at Louis Armstrong.
'And look here. One of the most famous
trumpet players.'

PÍO 'Which one is he?'

PUNTILLITA 'Who was the best trumpet ever?
The one who used to play out under the stars.
The guy who played the highest note ever at that time.'
Pío points at Ray Charles.

PÍO 'This one was blind. The great piano player.'
Puntillita points at Marilyn Monroe.

PUNTILLITA 'Look who else is here.
She seems famous, too.'

PÍO 'It says right here.
They sell everything in here.'
Pío points at John F. Kennedy.
'Who's the one in the middle?'

PUNTILLITA 'Which? The one with the saxophone?'

PÍO 'No, the one over here.'

PUNTILLITA 'Let's see if I remember his face.'

PÍO 'I can't remember ...'

PUNTILLITA 'He was one of the great leaders.
This is the life! The good life!'

Ibrahim

'I'd like you to know, this is the first time
that I find myself in New York, in the United States.
I've always longed to discover this city.
I'm not an American, nor can I speak English,
but I think that soon I'll learn a few words,
so I can hold my own.
How I'd love to bring
my wife and some of my kids
to see this.
So, they too, could see the beauty of it all.
This is very lovely.
Lovely, lovely, lovely.
Look there, Radio City.
At least, I'm getting to see it.

'I feel so happy seeing all of this.
I never could have imagined.
It's very beautiful.
Two years ago, or so,
I had decided to retire.
I didn't want to sing any more.
I was disillusioned.

I had to put up with too much.
The things of life.
I thought, "I'm bored with singing,
I'm not earning anything."

'As to this staff and my good fortune.
I tell you, it's my mother.
I've trusted in this staff for fifty-eight years.
That's how long I've had it;
that's how long she's been dead.'

Carnegie Hall

Music needs room to breathe

Ry Cooder in conversation with Peter Kemper

Let's start with some general questions. When I look back at your career as a working musician now for about thirty-five years, I get the impression that you are always searching for music which hasn't been corrupted?

To find music uncorrupted is at least to find music that starts with something, where something comes through; and I guess it turns out that what's trying to come through, whoever is doing it, is something about a place – I think that's really interesting. To think of it being corrupted means that the experience of the environment is washed away or erased by something else that gets in the way. I like places, I like music for or in a place – I think that's really interesting. When you hear music, right away you can tell if it's like living in the wrong town. It's an empty feeling, terrible. So what's appealing is not so much searching, it's just waiting for something that feels good, that you hear, that you know is really there; and it's not just a *menu du jour*, some kind of something cooked up for the day, you know. It's a process, something melting, boiling and thus getting a special flavour.

How do you deal with strange, nearly forgotten musical cultures that you want to document on records?

Well, if you're looking at the idea of documenting something, which is what a record or a book or a photograph does, then what you need to do is get as close as you can to the true centre of whatever that sound is. So you have to select. It's like saying, 'I like this song better than that song' or 'I like this guitar player better than that guitar player.' I don't think it has to do with technique and I don't think it even has to do with age so much, although age brings about more specific expression. A working musician who stays working is finally able to express more of that mysterious thing, you know, like a painter who paints and paints, and by picture ten thousand it's only a gesture. So, the more the master takes up his instrument the more freely it all comes out. But that takes time. What we don't have in the world, though, is time, because everybody is so compressed and sped up and hectic. When you see or hear something in which a lifetime has played a part, it's fantastic! It's like listening to the late Billie Holiday or something. People say, 'Oh I don't like the late Billie Holiday, it's too tortured, the voice is broken.' That's exactly right, it opens a window of her soul a little more. And there you have her broken life. It has nothing to do with artifice or style or the horrible sense of 'How do you like me now?' that you see all the time, winking and nodding: 'Here I am doing what I have to do.' You try to get away from it and find musicians who don't do that. It's not very easy!

Would you agree when we describe this ideal, let us say, as an ideal of 'innocent originality'?

Yeah, well you can say that, I guess. It's hard to know what to call it. Innocent is a tricky word, because that suggests 'naiveté' and I don't think that's quite the case. It's the wrong accent because experiences lead you away from simple naiveté. And there's something even deeper and more sublime. Having to do with knowing something – really, you need to know something [laughs].

You've sometimes mentioned the 'natural flow' of music. What does that mean for you? Is it the 'pulse' of the music, or how would you describe it?

Flow has something to do with the 'groove', it's a sensual feeling. There's a sort of centring, you know, in a flow that's right; it's like anything in nature that's in harmony, that's working right –

you can perceive it's harmonious and it's where it should be. It's not impeded by anything; you could say, it's nothing getting in the way. That's what 'flow' probably is.

I remember a sentence of yours: you've said, 'Music needs room to breathe.' Has that become impossible in Rock music today?

Yes, I think so. What happened is, the technology overtook the sentimental thing, the feeling of living. There was a time when the music and the technology were sort of parallel. But then greater technology influenced the music rather than the other way round. And I don't think that's good, because the music is not being served; but then again, something new is being created all the time, because technology turns out to be the big leader. It's like the engine that's pulling the train. So, we are pulled by technology every day of our lives. Look at all the people with mobile phones now, for instance. What are they doing? You listen to somebody saying 'Where are you now?' to their friend on the cell phone. 'Well, I'm outside this restaurant, I'm across the street.' So there's more and more of this weird, as Wim Wenders has said, 'second-hand experience', and third-hand experience through technology – it's so total. And when it comes to recorded music, then the music becomes stuck in the complexity of the technology, and that's what Rock 'n' Roll turned out to be. It didn't start that way.

Before we come to Cuba, let me ask some questions. Do you think that the song, the classical song structure, in its best sense – when telling a story – is that a threatened genre?

Yeah, hell, yes! Look at story-telling in films, for instance. People say, and I think it's true, that the need for narrative is a basic human drive, to codify information in the story form, like a song, a book, a film, a conversation, you know. So somewhere along the line people are going to reinvent ways of dramatic story-telling. But the trouble is, what stories are they going to tell, for Christ's sake? This is the thing that becomes very troublesome. I mean, it all started when the whole trend in modern culture was to make things louder and faster, and that's where the stories go, that's why you have action films and so forth. Or in Japan, where everything is more compressed than anywhere else in the world, they end up with movies that look like video games, and they invent video games. We are in such a goddam hurry all the time. Real stories, real narrative and real developments take time to experience. Speed has become the cultural ideal. But you can't speed up your experience unless you change yourself, give up

and become something else, like a character in a video game – that's what Rap music means to me, as an example of saying, 'I'm not going to be a person, really. I feel just like a weapon. I'm going to take away all the strange qualities that human beings have, the magical reality they might live in. And I'm going to reduce it down until it's just one element, like lead or carbon or something.' And that's what Rap does.

You once mentioned that you got about ninety per cent of your musical knowledge through hearing, seeing and jamming. Was it similar with the Cuban musicians? Were you familiar with Cuban music before?

Well, I was a bit familiar with the music. But I hadn't had the opportunity to play with Cubans; it's kind of a hard thing to get to do. But I listened to the records. We pay attention to these things, but you also have to know that you don't have anything until you get to where they are (they being anybody – might be Vietnamese, might be Moroccan, I don't know). You have to go somewhere where there is some consciousness that's unifying, and get to what that is. And that, of course, can only be expressed by a group. And there has to be a sufficient number of people to make up a group, so that you can begin to hear and feel things.

You may know the songs; I know the songs, I know who played them and made the records and I know the chord changes in the music, but that doesn't mean I know what's going on. It just means that I've logged a certain amount of listening time. But that's not the secret, it's only a step towards understanding. You've got to get with the people and you've got to sit there, and you have to have the opportunity to do it. I mean, you can't just phone up and say, 'Send me a bunch of Cubans.'

On some of your works with the Buena Vista Social Club you've played your electric slide guitar. Is there anything like a slide tradition in Cuba?

Oh no. I've never heard of it. The only person who recognized my slide playing was Compay Segundo, and he knew it was derived from Hawaiian. But the rest of the musicians don't know anything about the slide-guitar tradition. Compay did, because he knows a lot of stuff. He's ninety-two, he really knows everything. There's nothing he doesn't know [laughs]. Amazing really! He was there at the dawn of the whole thing, the rise of the Caribbean music and so on. It was great luck for me to meet him.

When I go back to the slide playing, do you still feel any kind of challenge in playing slide?

Oh, sure. I don't know how to describe it. It's a challenge to make a good sound, to move from one note to another, just floating to express something. Listen, the slide is just a tool to say something. It's a tiny little area to work in. You have to deal with microtones and so on – it's a case of 'less is more'. Great musicians play one note and you know: 'There it is! That's the note!' It only takes one note, and if you don't do it in that one, then you won't be able to do it in a million. It's very difficult, other than in the hands of somebody who is totally within whatever that scene is. I have met a few: Gabby Pahinui, Joseph Spence, Bill Johnson. But, as we know, masters are rare, like a grain of gold in the sand. How many are there ever? I mean, goddam, not very many. Although during the recording era (let's say, from 1910 to the present, or at least till 1980, maybe), which is what counts and matters, there's been a lot of people who have brought out so much good stuff because recording is an amazing phenomenon – so much and in so many fields. What then happened was, the playback came. The musician came in, he was recorded, then he heard himself back, and subconsciously made changes and adapted and perfected. And this is an interesting process, you know. Up to a point it really works perfectly, it's very efficient, perfecting and rendering down; then after a certain point it just becomes throwaway. The musician became a slave of the possibilities of changing a recording again and again. Look at Pop music! But then, some people have an incredible ability to keep reinventing themselves, to keep doing it. I mean, there's only a few, really.

Could the specific 'aura' or, let's say, 'quality' of Cuban son only survive in this limited and well-protected area, far away from the marketing thing?

Yeah, sure, of course! It survived in the way that Cuban music survived, in that it was a community music, music of the people. *Son* is a people's music rather than a commercial form. And as long as the culture is intact, it'll be alright. People will remember the songs, they know the songs; it's part of their world, you know. But I know a man in Hanoi, a Vietnamese musician, who is like

a Cuban – an old Cuban; he's like the Compay Segundo of Vietnam. And he told me that Vietnam was once a real beauty, a clear stream that's gotten muddied up. It's muddied up with all the commerce and all the other ideas and everything. This is an old man who lived because he couldn't fight in the war, because he was blind – fifty years of war after all, remember. He says, 'I'm the last.' I mean, that's a terrible thing to say about yourself. But it's what happens in the modern era. Cuba was so backward and so ignored and even avoided that the culture hung on a little bit longer, and their culture is strong. I mean, they have a specific sort of national unity about themselves, a feeling of brotherhood. And that really matters a lot. The poor Vietnamese undoubtedly had the same thing: they're a similar people – but what were they going to do with their country being blown up and burnt down, for Christ's sake? How is such a culture supposed to survive? What can be done? I hear this Vietnamese guy playing and I think it's one of the greatest tragedies – but it's just the way the world is.

Biographies of the musicians

Joachim Cooder
Drums

Joachim Cooder, son of Ry Cooder, was born in Santa Monica, California, in 1978. At the age of five the music of Jim Keltner made such a strong impression that he began to play the drums himself. Since then he has pursued many musical projects. In 1996 he accompanied his father and David Lindley on tour in Europe and Japan. He worked as co-producer on Ry Cooder's soundtrack compilation and as composer of the music for Mike Nichols' film *Primary Colors*. He played with Johnny Cash on the soundtrack for *Dead Man Walking* and with John Lee Hooker for his album *John Lee Hooker and Friends*. His band Speakeasy, with whom he has played in Los Angeles for three years, has been increasingly influenced by Joachim Cooder's experiences in Cuba.

Ry Cooder
Guitar

Born in 1947 in Los Angeles, California, Ry Cooder is a guitarist, composer and producer. He has earned a legendary reputation as a slide guitarist. He has played in Captain Beefheart's Magic Band, and has accompanied Gordon Lightfoot, the Rolling Stones, Eric Clapton, Randy Newman, John Lee Hooker and many others. Influenced from early on by blues, from the early 1970s he devoted himself to amplified musical traditions and became a pioneer of 'world music', when there was still no such term. He has worked in country and folk music, calypso, Hawaiian music, gospel, *salsa*, jazz, ragtime, and vaudeville music. Ry Cooder has composed soundtracks for more than twenty films. One of the best-known of his soundtracks was written for the film *Paris, Texas* (1985) by Wim Wenders, for whom he also wrote the music for the film *The End of Violence* (1998).

Bárbaro Alberto Torres Delgado, 'Barbarito Torres'
Laúd

'Barbarito', born in 1956, is probably the greatest Cuban master of the *laúd*, a twelve-stringed instrument similar to a lute. By the age of fourteen he was playing in a variety of orchestras. Today he also teaches music. He has appeared with top groups and musicians, including the guitarist Leo Brouwer, the pianist Papo Lucca and the famous Venezuelan *salsa* singer, Oscar de León.

Ibrahim Ferrer

Vocal

Ibrahim Ferrer was born during a local social club dance in 1927. Orphaned at the age of twelve, he sang on the streets and went on to found his first band with his cousin when he was thirteen. In the daytime he earned his living in a variety of ways so that he could sing at night. He came to the attention of the top orchestras of Santiago de Cuba and sang with them. From 1953 he worked with the Pacho Alonso group and in 1959 moved to Havana with them, where they called themselves Los Bocucos. He was known to other musicians, but for him – unlike the other members – the breakthrough only came with the Buena Vista Social Club. His dream of singing *boleros* came true when he recorded *Dos Gardenias*.

Rubén González

Piano

Rubén González, born in 1919, is one of the most influential of Cuban musicians. He was one of the trio of great pianists who developed the *mambo* and incorporated modern jazz harmonies into traditional Cuban music during the 1940s. His legendary piano playing has influenced the style of Cuban music for the past fifty years. He studied at the Cienfuegos Conservatory until 1934 and then went to medical school, leaving in 1941 to devote himself entirely to music. In the 1960s he teamed up with Enrique Jorrin, the inventor of the *cha-cha-cha*, with whom he remained associated for twenty-five years. In the 1980s, after Jorrin's death, Rubén briefly took over his band, but soon retired.

Pío Leyva

Vocal

Born in 1917 in Moron, Pío Leyva is one of the most prominent singers in the country, and he is known as 'El Montunero de Cuba'. At the age of six he won a bongo competition, and at fifteen he made his debut as a singer. Pío Leyva composed some of the best-known Cuban songs and is famous for his improvisations. He worked with the renowned bands of Benny More, Bebo Valdez and Noro Morales, and for a while he was a member of Compay Segundo y sus Muchachos. Since 1950 he has made twenty-five records. He also enjoys a strong following in West Africa, where in 1991 he went on tour for four months.

Manuel Licea, 'Puntillita'
Vocal

Born in 1927, Puntillita began to sing when he was seven years old, and by the age of fourteen he was a member of the Orchestra Liceo. He is a master of the entire range of Cuban song rhythms, especially the *son* and the *bolero*. In the 1950s he featured as one of Cuba's most popular singers with Havana's best-known orchestras, and he also worked with the legendary group Sonora Mantancera, started some seventy years ago.

Eliades Ochoa
Guitar, vocal

Eliades Ochoa, born in 1946, comes from a family of musicians. He began to sing and play the guitar at the early age of six. A quintessential *guajiro* (countryman or farmer), he never appears without his cowboy hat. At seventeen he ran his own radio show and in the 1970s he was the main attraction at the most popular music club in Santiago de Cuba. He took over as director of the Cuarteto Patria orchestra, a real Cuban institution, in 1978 and considerably expanded its repertoire, also taking it on tour outside Cuba. Eliades is one of the outstanding guitarists of his generation and plays on a nine-stringed instrument that he made himself.

Omara Portuondo
Vocal

Omara Portuondo, born in Havana in 1930, is regarded as Cuba's most expressive *bolero* singer. In 1952 she joined the Aida Diestro quartet and sang with it for fifteen years. She then pursued her solo career and now directs her own orchestra and goes on world tours. She has worked with Nat King Cole, Edith Piaf and others.

Compay Segundo
Vocal, guitar

Compay Segundo was born in 1907 as Francisco Repilado. In the daytime he worked in the tobacco fields and as a barber; in the evenings he played the guitar and clarinet in the bars of Santiago de Cuba, where he appeared with top Cuban musicians such as Sindo Garay and Nico Saquito. At the age of fifteen he wrote the first of his hundred or so compositions. In 1934 he moved to

Havana and performed in leading local orchestras. In 1942 he and Lorenzo Hierrezuelo founded the duo Los Compadres, which was to stay very successful for the next thirteen years: 'In our songs we addressed the simple things that the others didn't speak of. People liked the poetry of our music.... We didn't make a noise.' His nickname dates from that period: Compay is Cuban slang for *compadre* and Segundo refers to his trademark, bass harmony 'second' voice. He still performs today in the band he founded in 1956, Compay Segundo y sus Muchachos. He invented a seven-stringed instrument (the *armónico* or *trilina*), a combination of guitar and the Cuban *tres*, because he found the range of the *tres* too 'limited'.

Manuel Mirabal Vázquez, 'El Guajiro'
Trumpet, vocal

Manuel Mirabal Vázquez was born in 1933 and learned to play the trumpet from his father. He reached the height of his popularity in the 1950s: in 1953, he joined the jazz combo Swing Casino, and in 1956 he started his own band, Conjunto Rumbavana, and over this period he was also taken on by Havana's biggest orchestras as a singer. Manuel Mirabal, also known by his nickname 'El Guajiro',

played in the legendary group Sonora Mantancera, with which he also made recordings. He is a master of the entire range of Cuban rhythms, and has made a particular speciality of the *son* and the *bolero*.

Orlando López Vergara, 'Cachaíto'
Bass

Orlando, born in 1933, is continuing a family tradition, for the López family is almost a synonym of bass playing in Cuba. His father Orestes and his uncle Israel were taught by their father and in the 1930s the López brothers revolutionized bass playing in Cuba. Orestes played an important part in the birth of the *mambo*, Israel in the development of the *descarga* style. When his uncle, nicknamed 'Cachao', asked Orlando to stand in for him in the famous orchestra Arcana y sus Maravillas, Orlando, now known as 'Cachaíto', made such an impression that he was taken on as a permanent member. He is unusually versatile and is as happy to play Beethoven with the Orquestra Sinfonica Nacional as to play Cuban rhythms on electric bass and Latin American jazz on acoustic bass.

Film credits: Buena Vista Social Club

A film by Wim Wenders

A Road Movies production
in association with ARTE
and with the help of ICAIC

Executive Producer: *Uli Felsberg*
Associate Producer: *Rosa Bosch*
Produced by: *Uli Felsberg* and
Deepak Nayar

MUSICIANS
Octavio Calderón
Joachim Cooder
Ry Cooder
Angel Terry Domech
Ibrahim Ferrer
Ibrahim Ferrer Jr.
Manuel Galban
Roberto García
Hugo Garzón
Carlos González
Juan de Marcos González
Rubén González
Pío Leyva
Manuel 'Puntillita' Licea
Orlando 'Cachaíto' López
Eliades Ochoa
Gilberto 'Papi' Oviedo
Alejandro Pichardo
Yanko Pichardo
Omara Portuondo
Jesús 'Aguaje' Ramos
Salvador Repilado
José Antonio Rodríguez
Compay Segundo
Benito Suárez
Barbarito Torres
Alberto 'Virgilio' Valdés
Amadito Valdés

Manuel 'Guajiro' Mirabal Vázquez
Lázaro Villa

HAVANA CREW
Director of Photography
and Steadicam:
Jörg Widmer
Sound:
Martin Müller
Line Producer:
Rafael Rey Rodriguez
Focus Puller:
Julio Simoneau
Lighting:
Ivan Scull
Music Consultant:
Sigfredo Ariel
Assistant to Wim Wenders /
Translator: *Zita Marina Morrina Atia*

AMSTERDAM CREW
Director of Photography:
Robby Müller
Steadicam Operator:
Jörg Widmer
Camera Operators:
Claire Pijman
Theo Bierkens
Birgit Hillenius
Timecode Sync. Supervisor:
Rik Meier
Production Assistant:
Sven Sauèr

NEW YORK CREW
Unit Production Manager:
Linda Moran
Director of Photography:
Lisa Rinzler †
Camera Operator:
David Waterston

Assistant Camera:
Richard Rutkowski
Steadicam Operator:
Stephen Consentino
Stage Manager:
David Stahlbaumer
Lighting Designer:
Mitch Bogard
Production:
Luba Schatzberg

LOS ANGELES CREW
Editor:
Brian Johnson
Associate Editor:
Monica Anderson
Assistant Editor:
Gary Trentham
Post Production Supervisor:
Kristi Lake
Post Production
Sound Services:
Guaranteed Media
Sound Supervisor and
Re-recording Mixer:
Elmo Weber
Co-Supervisor and
Dialogue Editor:
Walter Spencer
ADR Supervisor and Mixer:
Russell Farmarco
On-line Editor:
Mark Sherman
Colorist:
Linda Olague
Encore Video Post Executive:
Michael Sable

BERLIN CREW
Legal Services Coordinator:
Kai-Peter Uhlig

Music Rights Clearance:
Steven Reich
Tax Advisor:
Erich Thum
Accounting:
Claudia Pauly
Vesna Rudinac
Ina Biallas
Project Coordinators:
Denise Booth
Rose-Marie Couture
Assistant to Wim Wenders:
Jolanda Darbyshire

All music recordings are copyright
World Circuit Limited

Original Concept and Executive
Producer of Recordings:
Nick Gold
World Circuit

Director of Marketing and
Artist Relations:
Jenny Adlington
World Circuit

Artistic Consultant:
Juan de Marcos González

All music recorded by:
Jerry Boys

All music mixed by:
Rail Rogut and *Ry Cooder*
at Ocean Way Studios

Filmed on
SONY DigiBetaCam and DV

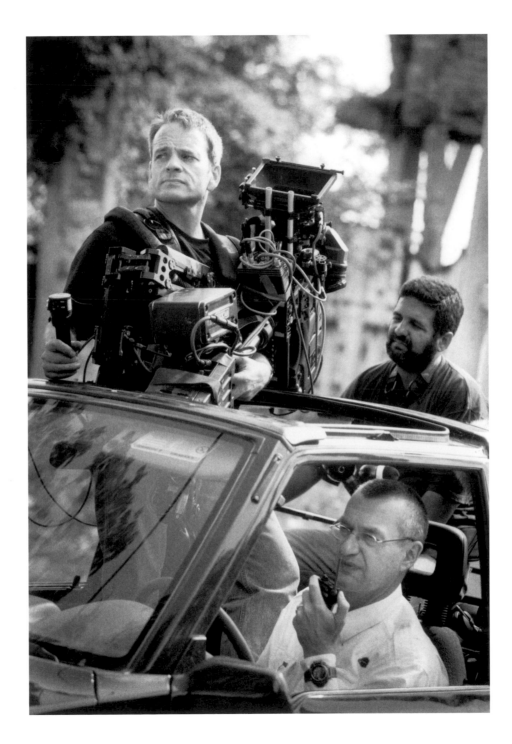

Nick Gold, music producer and publisher of World Circuit Records

Acknowledgments

We would like to express our special thanks to all those who have helped us in so many ways to create this book.

First and foremost, Susan and Ry, without whom we would never have gone to Havana in the first place. Uli and Deepak, who never ceased to believe in the film, even during its most difficult stages. Brian, who battled for a year with the heap of material until finally a film emerged from it.

Then Michel, for all his friendship and devotion to this book project. He was the first to support us in our idea of making a photographic book, and conjured wonderful prints out of sometimes very difficult negatives. Thanks also to his colleagues at A&I in Los Angeles: Paula, Ezra, Eleonora, Andrew, Eduardo and Jay, who often stayed late into the night working on each photograph with meticulous care and total dedication.

An enormous thank-you to In-Ah, who does everything to free our minds to think about such things as this book. For us, she is a true gift from the gods. Thanks to Patrick Lambertz, whose unerring eye helped to choose and print the images from the film. Also to Andrea, for her loyalty and for all the worries she has taken off our shoulders in recent years. She ran our office in Berlin single-handedly while we were shooting and editing. And to Carmen, who has always prepared a welcome home for us with her inexhaustible energy and loving eye for all our needs.

Thanks to our family, Barbara, Hella, Michael, Tamara, Alexa, Helmut and Friederike, who were and are always there for us, whatever the problems and doubts. Thanks to our friend and neighbour Michel, who has always 'come over' and who helped with the long-drawn-out process of the layout. Thanks to Cori, who, as a painter, gave wonderful advice; to Sylvie, who has a critical eye and who contributed much to the final result; to Jessica, whose enthusiasm for the photographs was an inspiration to us; and to Tanja, who spent hours and hours standing at the photocopier.

Thanks to Reinhard Penzel and Judith Reuter of SONY, who generously placed the necessary technology at our disposal.

Thanks to Robert Eisenhauer, Michael Donnelly and Bernard Eisenschitz.

And, last but not least, a very big thank-you to Lothar Schirmer, whose friendly and helpful advice and boundless optimism have led to what now lies before you. And to his colleague Claudia Rudeck, who has been a great help in the compilation and correction of the text.

Wim and Donata Wenders